Darwin and The First Grandfather:
A Story of Evolution

Darwin and The First Grandfather: A Story of Evolution

ERIKA K. HONORÉ AND PETER H. KLOPFER
WITH ILLUSTRATIONS BY GRETCHEN MORRISSEY

Copyright © 2016 Erika K. Honoré & Peter H. Klopfer
All rights reserved.

ISBN: 153538364X
ISBN 13: 9781535383646
Library of Congress Control Number: 2016912139
CreateSpace Independent Publishing Platform
North Charleston, South Carolina

Tim was a boy who just couldn't stop asking questions. Why do leaves turn yellow and fall off trees? How does the weatherman know it's going to snow tomorrow? Where do crystals come from? What will happen if I eat this caterpillar?

His friends usually rolled their eyes when Tim started with his questions, but they were interested in the answers too (especially the one about the caterpillar). At school, Ms. Douglas would wave her arms in the air and beg Tim to give someone else a chance to talk for a change! Tim asked a lot of questions at home too. His mom knew that he was genuinely curious about his world, so she always took time to try to explain things.

One night after dinner, Tim bounced into the living room looking for something to do. Mom was sitting on the couch sorting through a box of old photos. Tim didn't recognize any of the people in them. He pointed at a small, yellowish photograph. A little boy wearing shorts and knee socks sat on the lap of an old man with a round hat and a long white beard.

"Who's that boy, Mom?"

Mom looked at the photo and smiled.

"That's my grandfather, Nana's daddy, when he was little. The man he's with is his grandfather."

Tim frowned. He knew Nana, but couldn't remember meeting her father, or that man with the beard. Mom explained that these photos had been taken a long time ago, many years before Tim was born.

"So the old man is your grandfather's grandfather?"

"Yes, that's right."

"Do we have a picture of your grandfather's grandfather's grandfather?"

Mom laughed.

"No, I don't think we have one of those."

Somehow the idea of grandfathers having grandfathers was very funny to Tim. He tried to think back as far as he could, imagining a long line of grandfathers standing one after the other, grandfather after grandfather after.....hmmmm. Where did the line begin?

"Mom! Who was the first grandfather? What did he look like?" Where did he live? How did he get there? Where did he come from?

Mom laughed and put the photos down.

"Here we go again! Those are great questions, Tim, but I'm not sure I know all the answers."

She explained that people had been wondering for thousands of years about how humans, and animals too, had come to be on Earth. They made up stories about how it might have happened, trying to explain the things they saw. People all over the world came up with their own stories, and told them to their children. Tim jumped onto the couch next to her.

"Stories! Cool! Tell me, Mom! You know I love stories! And it's not nearly bedtime yet!"

Mom looked at her watch and sighed.

"Well, okay. Here's the deal. There are way more stories told all over the world than I've ever heard, but I'll tell two that I do know. Then you can decide for yourself which one you think gives the best answer to your questions."

Once upon a time, a very, very long time ago, there was no Earth, no moon, no sun, no stars. Then God, who was the most powerful being in the universe, created them all. He paid special attention to Earth. He covered Earth with grass, colorful flowers, all kinds of trees and rocks, sand and mud. He made the huge salty oceans, and the lakes and rivers, the mountains, the deserts, and the rolling plains. Earth was a beautiful place and He was very pleased with His work! Then He started making animals, birds, fish, insects and tiny invisible creatures to live on the beautiful planet. He made hundreds of different kinds, all colors, shapes and sizes. He made some to swim in the water, some to burrow in the earth, some to eat grass and others to eat fruit. He even made animals that would eat other animals!

When God was done, He sat back and thought for a while. He decided that all these thousands of animals needed a ruler to keep them in order. So, God made a special creation: a human. The first human He made was a man named Adam. God explained to Adam that he was special, different from all the other animals on earth. Adam was a good ruler, but he was lonely. To keep him company, God made another human, this time a woman named Eve. Eve and Adam were happy together on the beautiful planet, and they had some children. In time those children grew up and had children of their own, and those children did the same, until, after many, many years, the Earth was full of people.

Tim was quiet for a moment. Only a moment. Then he wiggled.

"So, Eve and Adam were the start of the line, and ALL of the people in the world came from them? Adam was the first grandfather?"

"Well," said Mom. "That's one story that a lot of people believe."

Tim wasn't satisfied.

"But we don't all look the same! My friend Gabi has brown skin and hair; Len's hair is black and curly, and my eyes are blue."

"That's a good point." Mom agreed. "Children usually look like the other people in their families. Gabi's parents come from Guatemala, and most people there have brown skin and dark hair and eyes like hers. Len's parents and grandparents grew up here, but his grandfather's grandfather came from Nigeria, where most people have hair, skin and eyes like his. Your grandparents came from England and Germany, and lots of people there have blue eyes and blond hair like you and me."

"But," objected Tim, "If they all started out from Adam and Eve, how come they ended up so different?"

Mom sighed and leaned back on the couch.

"Tim, do you remember Aunt Judy? She's a paleontologist; she studies fossils, very old bones and shells from animals that lived a long time ago."

Tim did remember. Aunt Judy brought him a little fossil of an animal called a trilobite. Mom explained that scientists like Aunt Judy are sort of like detectives, searching for clues from the past. They put all these clues together and try to find out what happened thousands or millions of years ago.

"OK", said Mom. "Now I'm going to tell you another story, about a boy who asked the same questions you did, but who used clues like Aunt Judy does to find the answers. The boy's name was Charles Darwin, and he lived in England about 150 years ago."

When Charles was young, his favorite thing was to be hiking and exploring, watching birds, chasing butterflies and collecting beetles. Charles was a good artist, and made careful drawings of the birds and animals he saw on his walks, and the plants and insects he collected. Since beetles were the easiest to catch, he was able to study them most closely. There were so many kinds! And all so different! Charles decided that God must have had a soft spot for beetles.

Charles also loved to visit the farm down the road from his home, especially in the spring when the new lambs and chicks were born. He filled his notebooks with drawings of them. One day he noticed something odd. A big brown hen was leading her brood of chicks out into the yard to scratch for bugs. Most of the chicks were fluffy tan blobs, just like their mother, but a couple were speckled brown and white. On the other side of the fence, white sheep were grazing while their white lambs butted and capered- but one of the lambs was grey, not white! Charles asked the farmer about them. The farmer shrugged and said it was just something that happened sometimes, and that the different colored babies were called "sports".

Tim interrupted. "Sports? Like games?"

"Well, in this case," explained Mom. "Sports is a word that scientists use to describe babies that look different from their parents, or their brothers and sisters."

Sometimes farmers chose to keep the sports instead of the normal-colored babies. In a few years, they had whole flocks of grey sheep and speckled hens. Charles began to wonder whether this could also happen without the farmer's choice. After all, spotted chicks nestled in the bushes might be harder for a hungry hawk to spot than solid tan or yellow ones. Maybe the sports had a better chance of survival? Maybe this was a natural process?

When Charles grew up, he went to university and learned as much as he could about biology, botany and the natural sciences. He still loved to roam the outdoors, observing and collecting plants and animals. He kept detailed journals of notes and drawings of the things he found on his walks, and studied them for hours. Then he got a fantastic opportunity! He was invited to go on a voyage around the world on a sailing ship called The Beagle. His job was to be Ship's Naturalist, describing all the new forms life the crew discovered along the way. It was the perfect job for him; Charles could hardly wait to set sail!

The Beagle voyage was everything Charles had hoped for, and more. He filled notebook after notebook with drawings and descriptions of the places he visited. One of the most fascinating places was a small group of islands off the coast of South America called the Galapagos. No humans or large mammals lived there, but the islands were covered with birds. These birds looked like the birds on the mainland of South America in many ways, but they were not exactly the same. Charles soon made the amazing discovery that each little island had its own special sort of plants and birds! The island that was covered in bushes with big, hard seeds had birds with thick, strong bills. The island that was draped in vines with cone-shaped flowers had birds with long, narrow bills. Charles could tell which island any bird came from just by looking at it!

Suddenly, Charles was struck with an idea. He remembered the farms he visited as a child, and the flocks of sheep and chickens with their sports. Maybe these birds were once all the same, and spread across all the islands. When sports hatched, maybe some were different colors like the lambs and chicks; but what if some of them had differently shaped bills instead? The sports with small bills would only be able to survive on an island that had plants with small, soft seeds that they could eat. Only sports with heavy bills would be able to crack the shells and eat on islands with large, thick seeds, and only those with long bills could reach down to the nectar in the cone-shaped flowers. It almost seemed as if nature had chosen certain sports on each island, just as the farmer had done with his flocks.

When the Beagle landed on the mainland of South America, Charles was able to do some more exploring. There he made another interesting discovery. Animals were all around him, hopping from rock to rock or grazing on the open grasslands. He carefully drew their pictures in his notebooks and described what he saw.

He also found lots of bones. Some were clearly the skeletons of the animals he was looking at, but others were very old and did not look quite the same. Charles noticed that the older the bones were, the more different they appeared from the recent skeletons.

Now this was fascinating! Charles knew that the lizards that lived a million years ago were different from the little lizards scampering over the rocks in front of him. There had been large ones and small ones, meat eaters and vegetarians. Probably some of the baby lizards were sports as well. Maybe some of the sports were faster runners, or could hide better than their brothers and sisters. Then they would have a better chance of survival, and would grow up to have babies themselves. In time, their babies would become the most common type of lizard. But if the environment changed, then other sports might do better. If it got a lot colder, then large dark lizards that could soak up the sunlight would be better able to survive than small, light ones. In this way, over thousands of years, the lizards would gradually seem to change. And, the skeletons left behind by the older kinds of lizards would look different from the newer ones.

By the time the Beagle finally sailed back to England, Charles had visited dozens of countries. He had filled stacks of notebooks with drawings and descriptions of the different animals he encountered; and people too. All of the people he met were humans, of course, and looked like him in a lot of ways. But, like the birds of the Galapagos Islands, people from other lands did not look quite the same. There were many variations in the color, shape and texture of skin, eyes, hair and other features. Charles wondered if these differences could be explained in the same way as the many sizes and shapes of the birds' bills. Was it possible that, like those birds, all humans once came from the same place and spread around the world from there?

Charles remembered that some scientists working in Africa had made an interesting discovery. They found some very old bones that looked a little like ape bones, and a little like human bones, but were slightly different from both. He let his imagination go, working on his new ideas. Perhaps, thousands of years ago, there were groups of these ape-like humans (or human-like apes) living in Africa.

Maybe some of their babies were sports. Some of the sports might have looked more like apes, with furry bodies and long arms for climbing. Others might have looked more like humans, walking on two legs and using their hands to carry things. Each of these sports would try to find a place to live where it could survive more easily than its parents, just like the birds with the different bills, or the lizards of many sizes and colors. The ape-like ones would do best in the forest, where they could climb trees. The human-like ones would have an easier time on the open plains where they could run. These sports would have babies that looked like them, and so large groups of both ape-like and human-like animals would be formed.

After many generations, and more sports, these groups would become more and more different. They would spread around the world into appropriate habitats. After a million years or so, we would clearly recognize some as apes and some as humans. The apes in different parts of the world would all resemble each other, but would not be quite the same. Some would be larger and heavier, some would have brown fur instead of black, some would have longer fingers. Some would live in trees, some on the ground. The same would be true for the humans. Blue eyes, brown eyes, curly hair, straight hair, skin color ranging from pale to dark; all different, but still clearly all humans.

Wow! Tim flopped back on the couch. His mind was churning, trying to process everything Mom had just told him. He had heard lots of stories, lots of ideas, lots of different explanations and answers to his questions. But somehow there was something special about Charles' ideas, something that made a lot of sense to Tim.

"Mom! Charles didn't just make up something that sounded good, did he? He looked for real clues, like a detective. Like Aunt Judy and other scientists do."

"That's right," Mom agreed. "And what's more, scientists have figured out ways to test some of Charles' ideas, to find out what really happened."

She explained that an idea that can be tested is called a theory. The idea that Charles had is called the Theory of Evolution. It says that if sports can survive better than their brothers and sisters (though this doesn't happen very often), there will be more and more of them. In this way, new kinds of animals appear.

"Charles called this Natural Selection. It's almost as if nature was choosing certain sports to live in each place, choosing the ones that could best live there and survive to raise their families."

Tim frowned. "But what about Adam and Eve? That was a good story too, but God made everything, all the people and all the animals and stuff. There's nothing in there about sports or evolution. "

Mom nodded. "Remember what I said at the start, Tim? People tell stories to try to explain how things happen. They tell those stories to their children, and write them in books. That story about Adam and Eve was written a very long time ago, long before Charles came up with his ideas. It is a special story that many, many people have heard and believe. In fact, it's the story that Charles grew up believing. But just because a story has been told for hundreds of years doesn't necessarily mean that things happened exactly that way. As you said, scientists look for clues that will help them figure out what happened millions of years ago. Those clues all tell us that Charles was right, and that the Theory of Evolution explains how people got here."

Tim had a funny idea. "So, the first grandfather was a monkey? EEE-EEE-EEE, OOO-OOO-OOO!" He started doing monkey-jumps on the couch. Mom grabbed him.

"Not exactly, though sometimes I think YOU are! Actually, scientists agree with Charles that both monkeys and humans evolved from the same ancestor, long, long ago.

"What's an ancestor? And what's evolved?"

"An ancestor is a member of your family that lived a long time ago, like the first grandfather. Evolved means they gradually changed, over thousands of years. OK, monkey boy, enough questions! The stories I just told you, and many more, can be found in books, Tim. I bet we can find some in the library tomorrow. But now……"

"I know, I know," groaned Tim.

"Bedtime!"

Made in the USA
Lexington, KY
03 April 2017